Becoming a Streamer

The Ultimate Guide

Maxime Luca

ISBN : 9798341236509

Publication Date: October 2024

Table of Contents

Introduction to Streaming

Streaming, short for "live streaming," is a form of digital media that has experienced explosive growth in recent years. It is a method of broadcasting video content in real-time over the internet, allowing creators to share their activities, skills, knowledge, or simply their daily lives with an online audience. Streaming has broadened the horizons of digital communication by enabling instant interaction between creators and their audience, transforming viewers into active participants.

What is Streaming ?

Streaming is distinct from traditional video broadcasting due to its real-time nature. Instead of uploading a pre-recorded video file, streamers broadcast their content live while viewers watch. This means that every action, reaction, comment, and event unfolds in real-time, creating an interactive and immersive experience.

Key elements of streaming include:

1. **Live Broadcasting**: The streamer uses streaming software to capture their screen, webcam, and audio in real-time and then

broadcasts it on a streaming platform. This broadcast is usually accompanied by a chat window where viewers can interact by asking questions, leaving comments, and sharing live reactions.

2. **Real-Time Interaction**: One of the most powerful features of streaming is the instant interaction between the streamer and the audience. Viewers can ask questions, provide feedback, and participate in polls in real-time, creating a direct connection with the content creator.

3. **Variety of Content**: Streaming is not limited to one type of content. Streamers can broadcast video games, sports events, talk shows, tutorials, live concerts, travel experiences, and much more. The diversity of content means that almost anyone can find a niche that suits them as a streamer.

4. **Online Community**: Streamers often build loyal communities of viewers who share common interests. These communities form around streaming channels, creating a space where people can connect, chat, and support one another.

5. **Monetization**: For some streamers, streaming can become a significant source of

income. Viewers can support creators by subscribing, donating, watching ads, or purchasing affiliate products, allowing streamers to earn money from their passion.

In summary, streaming is much more than just live video broadcasting. It is a social, interactive, and real-time experience that has the power to entertain, educate, bring communities together, and even create careers. Throughout this book, we will explore in detail how to become a successful streamer by providing practical advice and accurate information to guide you on your streaming journey.

The Rise of Streaming: Why It Matters

The rise of streaming has been one of the most significant phenomena of the digital age, and it is important for several essential reasons:

1. **Democratization of Content Creation**: Streaming has democratized content creation by allowing anyone with an internet connection and a camera to become a content creator. This means that diverse voices and perspectives can now be heard and seen, enriching the media landscape by offering a greater variety of content.

2. **Real-Time Interaction**: Streaming offers real-time interaction between creators and their audience. This instant interaction creates a sense of authenticity and connection that traditional media cannot replicate. Viewers can ask questions, provide feedback, and directly influence the content being broadcast, which strengthens community engagement and loyalty.

3. **New Career Opportunities**: Streaming has created new career opportunities in the field

of content creation. More and more people are able to make a living as streamers by monetizing their content through subscriptions, donations, advertising, and partnerships. This streaming economy has allowed many creators to pursue their passion and make a living from their art.

4. **Content Diversification**: Streaming is not limited to a single type of content. Streamers broadcast video games, sports competitions, live concerts, cooking shows, travel experiences, educational tutorials, and much more. This diversification means there is something for everyone, broadening the audience and encouraging creativity.

5. **Changing Media Consumption**: Streaming has contributed to changing how people consume media. Viewers are no longer limited to traditional television or fixed broadcast schedules. They can now choose what they want to watch, when they want, on a multitude of streaming platforms. This has disrupted the entertainment industry and forced major media companies to adapt.

6. **The Importance of Online Community**: Streamers often build engaged and loyal online communities. These communities can come together around common interests,

shared values, or simply the personality of the streamer. In times of social isolation, these communities can provide valuable support, friendship, and a sense of belonging.

In summary, the rise of streaming has profoundly changed how we create, consume, and interact with online media. It has expanded opportunities for creators, enhanced viewer engagement, and contributed to shaping modern digital culture. Understanding why streaming matters is essential for anyone looking to get involved in this ever-evolving field.

The Different Streaming Platforms (Twitch, YouTube Gaming, etc.)

The landscape of streaming platforms is rich and diverse, offering streamers a variety of options for sharing their live content. Each of these platforms has its own features, advantages, and disadvantages, making it essential to choose one that aligns best with your goals and streaming style. Here's an overview of some of the most popular streaming platforms:

1. **Twitch**: Twitch is one of the most iconic streaming platforms, primarily focused on video gaming, although it has expanded its content to include categories like music, art, cooking, and much more. It is known for its active community and robust monetization features, including subscriptions, bits (a virtual currency), and brand partnerships.

2. **YouTube Gaming**: YouTube Gaming is a branch of YouTube dedicated to live gaming content and game videos. It benefits from YouTube's enormous audience, which can be an advantage for streamers looking to reach a broader audience. Revenue comes from ad revenue, donations, and YouTube Premium subscriptions.

3. **Kick**: Kick is a streaming platform that takes cues from Twitch and YouTube Gaming.

4. **Facebook Gaming**: Facebook Gaming has rapidly developed as a streaming platform, leveraging Facebook's large user base. Streamers can reach an audience already present on Facebook, and viewer donations are managed through Facebook Stars. Monetization is also possible through ads and collaborations.

5. **Trovo Live**: Trovo Live is an emerging streaming platform focused on building a community of streamers and viewers. It offers features like virtual gifts and subscriptions for content creators.

6. **Other Specialized Platforms**: There are also specialized streaming platforms for specific niches. For example, Caffeine focuses on live

gaming and entertainment, while YouNow is popular for vlog-style streams and live music.

The choice of platform will depend on your goals as a streamer, your target audience, your content style, and your monetization strategy. It is important to conduct thorough research on each platform, observe what other streamers are doing, and consider how you can stand out on the one you choose. Once you have selected a platform, it's time to create an account, customize your channel, and start broadcasting your content live to build your audience.

Chapter 1

Preparation Before Starting

Assessing Your Interests and Skills

Success as a streamer begins long before you hit the "Start Streaming" button. Before diving into the world of streaming, it's essential to prepare properly. A crucial step in this preparation is evaluating your interests and skills. Here's why it's so important and how to do it effectively:

Evaluating Your Interests:

1. **Finding Your Passion:** Streaming is an adventure that requires time and commitment. The first step is to identify what you are passionate about. This could be video games, cooking, music, technology, travel, beauty, or any other area that attracts you. Choosing a subject that excites you will help keep you motivated over time.

2. **Considering Your Target Audience:** Think about your ideal audience. Who would you like to reach and entertain with your content? Understanding your target audience will help you tailor your content and streaming style to meet their needs and interests.

3. **Analyzing the Competition:** Look at other streamers who cover similar topics. This will give you an idea of what is already working on your chosen platform and what you could do differently to stand out.

Evaluating Your Skills:

1. **Identifying Your Strengths:** Reflect on your current skills and talents. Perhaps you are an exceptional player in a specific game, a talented musician, or an expert in cooking. Use your strengths to create unique and engaging content.

2. **Working on Your Weaknesses:** Also, identify your weaknesses. If you're not comfortable in front of a camera or have technical gaps, don't worry. Streaming is also an opportunity for continuous learning. You can acquire new skills as you progress along your journey.

3. **Building Your Online Presence:** Having a strong online presence, including on social media, can be a valuable asset for a streamer. If you don't yet have accounts on major social platforms, this may be the time to create them and start building your community.

When assessing your interests and skills, remember that streaming is not just for experts. You can progress and improve along the way. The key is to start with a solid foundation by choosing a field that you are passionate about and leveraging your personal strengths. This will help you create authentic and engaging content that attracts a loyal audience.

Choosing a Streaming Niche

Choosing a streaming niche is a critical step to succeed as a streamer. A niche defines the main subject or theme of your streaming channel and helps attract a specific target audience. Here's why it's important and how to choose the right niche:

Why Choosing a Niche is Important:

1. **Defining Your Online Identity:** Your streaming niche is essential for defining who you are as a content creator. It creates a clear image of what viewers can expect from your channel, helping you stand out in a sea of streamers and establishing your unique online identity.

2. **Reaching a Specific Audience:** Selecting a niche allows you to target a specific audience that is already interested in the topic you are covering. This increases your chances of creating an engaged and loyal community.

3. **Facilitating Content Creation:** By choosing a niche that you are passionate about, you'll be more motivated to create content regularly.

You'll also have more knowledge about the subject, which will help you provide quality content.

4. **More Effective Monetization:** A well-chosen niche can also facilitate the monetization of your channel. Viewers interested in your niche are more likely to subscribe, donate, and support your channel financially.

How to Choose the Right Streaming Niche:

1. **Review Your Interests and Skills:** Think about what excites you and what you do well. The best niches are often those that align with your passions and strengths.

2. **Research the Competition:** Look at what other streamers are doing in similar niches. Is there space for you to stand out or offer something different? Analyze what works well for others and what could be improved.

3. **Identify Your Target Audience:** Who are you most likely to reach with your niche? What are their interests and needs? Consider creating content that meets those expectations.

4. **Test and Adjust:** Keep in mind that your niche can evolve over time. Don't hesitate to test different types of content at the start to see

what works best. You can adjust your niche based on audience reactions.

5. **Stay Consistent:** Once you've chosen a niche, stay consistent. Viewers like to know what to expect from you. Create a regular streaming schedule and continue to explore topics related to your niche.

Ultimately, choosing a streaming niche that excites you and fits your personality is key to success. Your enthusiasm will shine through on screen, attracting an engaged and loyal audience. Don't be afraid to experiment and adjust your niche as you evolve as a streamer.

Equipment Needed to Get Started (Streaming Equipment, Computer, Internet Connection, etc.)

When deciding to become a streamer, one of the first crucial steps is to gather the necessary equipment to ensure quality broadcasts. The right gear is essential for providing a smooth and professional streaming experience. Here's a list of essential items and recommendations for each category:

1. **Computer:** Your computer is the heart of your streaming operation. It needs to handle real-time video processing. Minimum specifications depend on the type of content you plan to stream, but here are some general recommendations:

o **Processor:** A powerful processor is crucial. Multi-core processors like the Intel Core i7 or AMD Ryzen series are preferred.

o **Graphics Card:** A decent graphics card is important for handling live graphics. Nvidia GeForce or AMD Radeon graphics cards offer good performance.

o **RAM:** The more RAM you have, the better. At least 16GB of RAM is recommended.

o **Storage:** Use an SSD (Solid State Drive) for your operating system and applications for better responsiveness.

2. **Internet Connection:** A fast and stable Internet connection is crucial for live streaming. Here are some recommendations:

o **Download Speed:** A download speed of at least 5 Mbps is the bare minimum, but for optimal quality, 10 Mbps or more is recommended.

- **Upload Speed:** An upload speed of at least 3 Mbps is generally required for quality HD streaming.

- **Wired Connection:** If possible, use a wired Ethernet connection instead of Wi-Fi for a more stable connection.

3. **Streaming Equipment:** Streaming equipment includes the gear necessary to capture, record, and broadcast your content live. The main items are:

   - **Camera:** A quality webcam is important for showing your face live. Popular options include the Logitech C920 or Logitech Brio.

   - **Microphone:** A good microphone will significantly enhance your audio quality. The Blue Yeti, Audio-Technica AT2020, or Shure SM7B are popular choices.

   - **Capture Card:** If you plan to stream games from a console, a capture card like the Elgato HD60 S is necessary.

   - **Lighting:** Good lighting is essential for a clear appearance on screen.

Affordable LED lighting kits are available.

- o **Stands and Accessories:** A webcam stand, microphone arm, green screen (chroma key) for overlays, and other accessories may be useful depending on your streaming style.

Make sure to research the specifications and reviews for each component to ensure they meet your specific needs.

In summary, the equipment needed to start streaming includes a powerful computer, a fast and stable Internet connection, and quality streaming gear such as a webcam, microphone, and other accessories. Investing in quality equipment can significantly enhance the quality of your live broadcasts and make your content more appealing to viewers.

Chapter 2

Setting Up Your Streaming Channel

Creating an Account on the Streaming Platform

Setting up your streaming channel is an essential step for starting out as a streamer. This chapter will focus on the first step: creating an account on the streaming platform of your choice. Here's how you can proceed:

Creating an account on the streaming platform:

1. **Choose Your Platform:** Before creating an account, decide which streaming platform you want to broadcast on. The most popular platforms include Twitch, Kick, YouTube Gaming, Facebook Gaming, and others.

2. **Prepare Necessary Information:** You will need to provide certain information to create an account. This generally includes a username, an email address, a password, and sometimes payment information for monetization earnings.

3. **Review the Terms of Service:** Before clicking "Create Account," take the time to read the

platform's terms of service. Make sure you understand the rules and policies to avoid any future issues.

4. **Create Your Account:** Follow the steps to create your account. Choose a username that is easy to remember and reflects your streaming channel. Also, ensure that your password is secure.

5. **Customize Your Profile:** Once your account is created, customize your profile by adding a profile picture, a banner, and an appealing description. This will help viewers learn more about you and your content.

6. **Set Up Security Settings:** Security is important. Configure your account's security settings to protect your content and audience. This may include enabling two-factor authentication and managing privacy settings.

7. **Download the Streaming Software or App:** Depending on the platform you've chosen, you may need to download specific streaming software or an app. This will allow you to set up the capture of your screen, webcam, and microphone.

8. **Log Into Your Streaming Account:** Once you have installed the streaming application, log into your account using your credentials.

9. **Customize Streaming Settings:** Before you start streaming live, take the time to customize the streaming settings according to your preferences. This may include video resolution, bitrate, and keyboard shortcuts.

10. **Familiarize Yourself with the Dashboard:** Each streaming platform has a dashboard where you can manage your channel, interact with viewers, and access statistics. Familiarize yourself with these tools for effective channel management.

Once your account is created and your channel is set up, you'll be ready to start streaming live. The account creation process may vary slightly from platform to platform, but these general steps will help you get on the path to streaming.

Customizing Your Channel (Name, Logo, Banner, Description, etc.)

Customizing your streaming channel is a crucial step to stand out and attract a loyal audience. A well-designed and aesthetically pleasing channel can have a significant impact on the first impression viewers have of you. Here's how to effectively customize your streaming channel:

1. **Choose a Memorable Channel Name:** Your channel name is one of the first elements viewers will see. It should be memorable, reflect the content you provide, and be easy to remember. Ensure that your channel name is unique and does not infringe on copyrights or trademarks.

2. **Create a Distinctive Logo:** A logo is an image that represents you. It should be simple, distinctive, and suitable for your niche. A good logo can help strengthen brand

recognition. You can create it yourself if you have graphic design skills, or hire a graphic designer to get a professional logo.

3. **Design an Eye-Catching Banner:** Your channel banner is a large image that appears at the top of your profile. Use this space to display your logo, write your channel name, and add visual elements that reflect your style or content. Make sure the banner is high resolution for a clear appearance.

4. **Write an Engaging Channel Description:** Your channel description is where you can briefly explain what viewers can expect from your content. Use this space to describe your niche, your streaming days and times, your goals, and to add links to your social media or website (if you have one).

5. **Use Custom Panels:** Most streaming platforms allow you to create custom panels that appear under your video stream. Use these panels to provide additional information about yourself, your channel rules, your partners, and other relevant details. You can also include links to your social media and calls to action, such as subscribing or donating.

6. **Maintain Visual Consistency:** Make sure all elements of your channel, from the logo to the banner to the panels, follow a cohesive theme or visual style. This will help create a strong and professional brand image.

7. **Update Regularly:** Don't neglect to update your channel. If your logo, banner, or description changes, make sure to update these elements to reflect those changes.

Customizing your streaming channel is an ongoing process. Take the time to think about how you want to present yourself and invest in an aesthetic that matches your style and content. A well-customized channel can help attract a loyal audience and give your channel a professional look.

Configuring Streaming Settings (Resolution, Bitrate, etc.)

Configuring your streaming settings is an essential step to ensure a high-quality live broadcast. These settings determine the video resolution, audio quality, and overall stability of your stream. Here are some key parameters to consider when setting up your stream:

1. **Video Resolution:** The video resolution determines the clarity of your live video. Common resolutions include 720p (HD), 1080p (Full HD), and even 4K for streamers with more powerful equipment. The choice of resolution will depend on your hardware and the platform you are using. The higher the resolution, the more bandwidth is required.

   o **Tip:** Choose the highest resolution that your hardware and internet connection can handle without causing slowdowns.

2. **Bitrate:** The bitrate controls the overall quality of your live broadcast. It determines the amount of video and audio data you send to the streaming platform. A higher bitrate means better quality, but it also requires a faster internet connection.

   o **Tip:** Use a bitrate suitable for your internet connection. A bitrate of 3,000 to 6,000 Kbps is generally sufficient for HD quality.

3. **Frames Per Second (FPS):** The frame rate represents the number of frames displayed per second in your stream. Most streamers use 30 or 60 FPS. A rate of 60 FPS gives a smoother appearance to your broadcast but also requires more processing power.

   o **Tip:** Choose a frame rate that corresponds to the smoothness of your content. Fast-paced games may benefit from 60 FPS, while other content may work well at 30 FPS.

4. **Video and Audio Codec:** The video and audio codecs you use affect the quality of your content. Popular codecs include H.264 for video and AAC for audio. Most streaming software offers options to select codecs.

o **Tip:** Use the codecs recommended by the streaming platform you are using for optimal compatibility.

5. **Audio Preferences:** Make sure your audio preferences match your equipment. You can choose the source of your microphone, adjust the volume, and enable noise reduction if necessary.

o **Tip:** Test your audio before going live to ensure it is clear and distortion-free.

6. **Advanced Streaming Options:** Some streaming platforms offer advanced options such as using a custom streaming server (if you are an advanced streamer), enabling local backup of your broadcast, and other specific settings.

o **Tip:** Familiarize yourself with the advanced options in your streaming software, but only modify them if you fully understand how they work.

Correctly configuring your streaming settings ensures a high-quality streaming experience for your viewers. Feel free to test and adjust to find the setup that works best for your hardware, internet connection, and content style. The quality of your broadcast is a key factor in attracting and retaining your audience.

Chapter 3

Content Creation

Planning Your Content

Content creation is at the heart of streaming. It's why viewers turn to your channel and choose to follow you. In this chapter, we will cover the first essential step of content creation: planning. Here's how to effectively plan your streaming content:

Planning Your Content:

1. **Define Your Goals:** Before you start planning your content, clearly identify your objectives as a streamer. What do you want to achieve with your channel? You might want to entertain, educate, inform, or simply share your passion. Your goals will influence the type of content you create.

2. **Know Your Audience:** Understand who your target audience is. What are their interests, needs, and expectations? Knowing your audience will help you create content that resonates with them and build an engaged community.

3. **Choose a Niche:** If you haven't already chosen a niche, now is the time to do so. A niche defines the main subject of your

content, allowing you to target a specific audience. Make sure your niche aligns with your interests and those of your audience.

4. **Create a Streaming Schedule:** Establish a regular streaming schedule. Specify the days and times you will go live. Consistency is essential for building a loyal audience.

5. **Plan Themes and Topics:** For each live stream, plan in advance the themes and topics you will cover. Ensure you have enough content for the duration of the stream.

6. **Create a Script or Key Points:** To keep your stream flowing smoothly, it may be helpful to create a script or note some key points you want to address. This will help you stay organized and avoid awkward silences.

7. **Integrate Audience Interaction:** Encourage live interaction by responding to viewers' comments and questions. Schedule moments to engage with your audience throughout the stream.

8. **Vary Your Content:** Avoid streaming the same thing every time. Vary your content by offering different categories, special guests, challenges, Q&A sessions, etc.

9. **Analyze Past Performance:** Use data from your previous streams to understand what works best. What are the most popular moments? Which topics attract the most audience? Use this information to refine your planning.

10. **Stay Flexible:** While planning is important, be ready to adapt to live events. Sometimes, spontaneous moments can become the most memorable.

Planning your streaming content will help you maintain an efficient workflow, achieve your goals, and provide a consistent streaming experience for your viewers. Remember that planning doesn't have to be rigid, and don't be afraid to experiment and adjust your content based on your audience's reactions.

Interactivity with Your Audience

Interactivity with your audience is one of the most powerful features of live streaming. It allows you to create a real connection with your viewers, foster audience loyalty, and provide a more engaging streaming experience. Here's why interactivity is important and how you can incorporate it into your streaming content:

Why Interactivity is Important:

1. **Builds an Engaged Community:** When you regularly interact with your viewers, you involve them more in your channel. This can foster the creation of an engaged community of fans who return regularly to watch and interact with you.

2. **Personalizes the Experience:** Interactivity allows you to personalize the viewing experience for each viewer. You can respond to their questions, greet newcomers, and even take their suggestions into account for future content.

43

3. **Improves Retention:** Viewers are more likely to stay on your channel and watch for longer periods if you actively engage them. An engaged audience is also more likely to share your content with others.

4. **Creates Memorable Moments:** Interactive moments, such as live reactions to donations or comments, can create memorable experiences for your viewers. They will feel connected to you and your channel in a unique way.

How to Incorporate Interactivity into Your Streaming Content:

1. **Read and Respond to Live Comments:** Monitor viewer comments in real-time and respond during your stream. Ask questions to encourage viewer participation.

2. **Q&A Sessions:** Schedule specific times when you respond to viewer questions. This can be done regularly or during dedicated Q&A sessions.

3. **Play with Viewers:** If you're playing video games, consider playing with your viewers. You can host online matches with them,

invite them to join your games, or even create community tournaments.

4. **Contests and Giveaways:** Organize contests or live giveaways to reward your loyal viewers. Prizes can include virtual gifts, sponsored products, or niche-related items.

5. **Invite Viewers as Guests:** Occasionally, invite viewers to join you as special guests during your streams. This creates direct interaction and enhances the sense of community.

6. **Ask for Audience Feedback:** Encourage your viewers to provide honest feedback on your content and channel. This can help you improve your content and better meet your audience's expectations.

7. **Be Authentic:** Authenticity is key to interactivity. Be yourself, be natural, and show interest in your viewers. This will help establish a genuine connection.

Interactivity with your audience can take many forms, so don't hesitate to experiment and find what works best for your channel and streaming style. Ultimately, the more you engage with your audience, the more likely your streaming channel will thrive.

Content Quality: Entertainment and Added Value

The quality of the content you offer during your live streams is crucial for attracting and retaining your audience. When you stream live, you need to entertain your audience and provide them with real added value. Here's why content quality is essential and how to improve it:

Why Content Quality is Important:

1. **Attracts and Retains Viewers:** Content quality is the main factor that encourages viewers to choose to follow you and return to watch your future streams. Quality content will attract a loyal audience.

2. **Differentiates Your Channel:** In a world where thousands of streamers are available on different platforms, the quality of your content is what sets you apart. It creates a unique identity for your channel.

3. **Engages the Audience:** Quality content actively engages the audience, resulting in comments, live discussions, and an interactive viewing experience. This strengthens the bond between you and your viewers.

4. **Facilitates Monetization:** If you plan to monetize your channel, quality content is essential. Viewers are more likely to donate, subscribe, or watch ads if your content is entertaining and informative.

How to Improve the Quality of Your Content:

1. **Planning and Preparation:** Take the time to plan your live streams. Have a clear objective for each stream and prepare accordingly. A good script or list of key points can help you stay on track.

2. **Audience Interaction:** Actively respond to comments and questions from your audience during the live stream. Create an interactive environment where viewers feel heard and appreciated.

3. **Audio and Video Quality:** Invest in good audio and video equipment to ensure

optimal quality. Clear sound and sharp video significantly enhance the viewing experience.

4. **Original and Creative Content:** Strive to create original and creative content that stands out. Don't hesitate to explore new ideas and propose unique formats.

5. **Personal Presentation:** Be yourself on screen. Your personality and authenticity are major assets. Create a connection with your audience by showing your passion for the content you stream.

6. **Narrative Structure:** Use effective narrative structure to capture your audience's attention. Start strong, maintain interest throughout the stream, and end on a memorable note.

7. **Continuous Learning:** Be willing to learn and improve. Analyze the performance of your past streams, gather feedback from your audience, and adjust your content accordingly.

8. **Plan Special Moments:** Create special moments during your streams, such as events, special guests, challenges, or giveaways for viewers. These moments can create memorable experiences.

9. **Stay Informed:** Keep up with trends in your niche and the streaming platform you are using. This will enable you to create relevant and current content.

By combining entertainment and added value, you can create high-quality streaming content that attracts and retains your audience. Be passionate about what you do, be authentic, and continuously seek ways to improve your content. This will contribute to the growth of your channel and the creation of an engaged community.

Chapter 4

Establishing an Online Presence

Promoting Your Streaming Channel on Social Media

In this chapter, we will explore the importance of promoting your streaming channel on social media. Establishing a strong online presence outside of your main streaming platform is essential for attracting a broader audience and retaining your existing viewers.

Promoting Your Streaming Channel on Social Media:

1. **Choose the Right Platforms:** There are many social media platforms, and it's crucial to select the ones that best suit your content and audience. Popular platforms for streamers include Twitter, Instagram, Facebook, TikTok, and Discord.

2. **Create Consistent Profiles:** Ensure that your social media profiles reflect the aesthetic of your streaming channel. Use the same

username, profile picture, banner, and description to create consistency.

3. **Share Clips and Highlights:** Use your social media to share clips from your live streams and highlights of your content. Show your followers what they can expect from your channel.

4. **Schedule Your Posts:** Create a regular posting schedule to maintain consistent engagement with your audience. Plan posts to promote your upcoming live streams, share news related to your channel, and interact with your followers.

5. **Use Relevant Hashtags:** Research relevant hashtags related to your niche and content. Including popular hashtags can help your posts reach a wider audience.

6. **Collaborate with Other Creators:** Collaborating with other streamers or content creators can help you expand your audience. You can host joint streams or special events.

7. **Host Contests and Giveaways:** Contests and giveaways on social media can encourage people to subscribe to your streaming channel. Offer attractive rewards and encourage participation.

8. **Engage with Your Community:** Respond to comments, direct messages, and mentions on social media. Engaging with your community strengthens bonds and creates a more loyal fanbase.

9. **Post Exclusive Content:** To entice people to follow you on social media, offer exclusive content, such as behind-the-scenes previews, special announcements, and insider information.

10. **Avoid Over-Promotion:** While it's important to promote your channel, make sure not to overdo it to the point of overwhelming your followers. Balance your promotional posts with authentic and entertaining content.

11. **Analyze the Data:** Use the analytics provided by social media platforms to understand what works best in terms of promotion. Adapt your strategy based on data and audience feedback.

Promoting your streaming channel on social media is a key element in growing your audience. It allows you to reach new viewers and maintain ongoing engagement with your existing community. Invest time in managing your social media accounts and ensure you create an online presence that reflects the personality of your streaming channel.

Collaborating with Other Streamers

Collaborating with other streamers is a powerful strategy for growing your streaming channel, expanding your audience, and creating beneficial synergies for all participants. Here's why collaboration is important and how you can approach it effectively:

Why Collaboration with Other Streamers is Important:

1. **Expanding Your Audience:** When you collaborate with other streamers, you expose your content to their audience and vice versa. This can help you attract new viewers interested in your niche.

2. **Creating Unique Content:** Collaborations can lead to the creation of unique and entertaining content. The interaction between different streamers can be both entertaining and informative for viewers.

3. **Strengthening Community Bonds:** Collaborations reinforce connections within

the streaming community. Viewers often enjoy seeing their favorite streamers work together, which can foster loyalty.

4. **Diversifying Content:** You can expand the variety of your content by collaborating with other streamers who have different skills or interests. This can keep your channel fresh and interesting.

How to Approach Collaboration with Other Streamers:

1. **Identify Compatible Streamers:** Look for other streamers whose content or niche complements yours. They should have a similar or compatible audience.

2. **Reach Out:** Contact the streamers you wish to collaborate with through social media, direct messages, or emails. Explain your collaboration proposal and highlight the mutual benefits.

3. **Plan Together:** A successful collaboration requires prior planning. Discuss the date, time, and type of content you will create together. Ensure that expectations are clear.

4. **Integrate Your Audiences:** During the collaboration, encourage your respective

audiences to join in. Use mentions and links to direct viewers to your collaborator's channel.

5. **Stay Open to Adaptation:** Be flexible and open to your collaborator's ideas. Sometimes, spontaneous moments can be the most memorable.

6. **Promote the Collaboration:** Before the collaboration and during the live stream, promote the event on your social media, your channel, and other platforms.

7. **Ensure Good Technical Quality:** Make sure that the live stream quality is optimal, both in terms of audio and video. Technical issues can ruin a collaboration.

8. **Be Respectful and Professional:** Follow the rules of the streaming platform and treat your collaborator with respect. A successful collaboration relies on communication and professionalism.

9. **Analyze the Results:** After the collaboration, review the performance and audience feedback. This will help you evaluate the impact of the collaboration and plan for future collaborations.

Collaborating with other streamers can be a rewarding experience for both you and your audience. Look for collaboration opportunities that match your content style and goals, and don't be afraid to explore new ideas for innovative collaborations.

Building an Online Community

Building an online community is a crucial step for long-term success as a streamer. A loyal community can not only support you financially but also create a positive atmosphere around your streaming channel. Here's why building an online community is important and how you can effectively develop it:

Why Building an Online Community is Important:

1. **Audience Retention:** A strong, engaged community is more likely to return regularly to watch your live streams. Audience retention is essential for long-term success.

2. **Financial Support:** An online community can support your channel financially through donations, paid subscriptions, merchandise purchases, and ad revenue. The larger your community, the more significant these revenue sources can potentially be.

3. **Content Sharing:** An active community is more likely to share your content with others,

contributing to the expansion of your audience.

4. **Creating a Positive Atmosphere:** By building an online community, you have the opportunity to create a positive and welcoming atmosphere around your channel. This attracts new viewers and encourages existing viewers to stay.

How to Develop an Online Community:

1. **Be Consistent:** Maintain a regular streaming schedule so your audience knows when you are online. Consistency creates expectations and encourages viewers to return.

2. **Engage Actively:** Respond to viewers' comments and questions during the live stream. Create an interactive environment where viewers feel heard and appreciated.

3. **Create a Community Space:** Use platforms like Discord to create a space where your viewers can chat, share information, and connect with one another. A Discord server can become the heart of your community.

4. **Organize Community Events:** Regularly organize special events or activities to involve your community. This can include gaming

sessions with viewers, contests, or Q&A sessions.

5. **Recognize and Reward:** Thank and reward your loyal viewers. You can designate "moderators" to manage the chat, offer special badges to subscribers, or even host special events for community members.

6. **Create a Community Culture:** Establish community rules to maintain a positive and respectful environment. Encourage mutual respect among community members.

7. **Get Involved Outside of Live Streams:** Be active on social media and interact with your community outside of live streams. Share updates, anecdotes, and moments from your personal life.

8. **Listen to Feedback:** Be open to feedback from your community. Audience input can help you improve your content and better meet their expectations.

9. **Special Events and Celebrations:** Organize special events to celebrate milestones for your channel, such as streaming anniversaries or subscriber goals reached.

10. **Be Authentic:** Be yourself and be authentic in your interactions with your community.

Transparency and authenticity strengthen trust and the bond between you and your viewers.

Building an online community takes time and effort, but the long-term benefits are worth it. Be patient, engage actively with your audience, and create an environment where viewers feel valued and respected. A strong community is one of the most valuable assets you can have as a streamer.

Chapter 5

Managing Live Streaming

Preparation Before Each Live Stream

In this chapter, we will discuss managing live streaming, focusing on preparation before each broadcast. Careful preparation is essential to ensure that your streams run smoothly and provide a high-quality experience for your audience.

Preparation Before Each Live Stream:

1. **Check Your Equipment:** Before starting your broadcast, ensure that all your equipment is functioning properly. Check your camera, microphone, lighting, and any other gear you are using. Conduct audio and video tests to guarantee optimal quality.

2. **Test Your Internet Connection:** A stable internet connection is crucial for live streaming. Ensure that your connection is fast and reliable enough to support the resolution and bitrate you plan to use.

3. **Set Up Your Streaming Space:** Create a clean and organized environment for your live stream. Make sure your space is well-lit and

free from distracting visual or auditory interruptions.

4. **Load Your Resources:** If you use graphics, videos, or slides during your stream, ensure they are loaded and ready to go. Organize your files for easy access.

5. **Prepare Your Content:** Review your content plan and key points for the live stream. If you have special segments, guests, or events planned, make sure they are well-prepared.

6. **Test Your Streaming Software:** Ensure that your streaming software is set up correctly. Check your resolution settings, bitrate, audio and video sources, and conduct an unlisted live test stream to verify that everything works as expected.

7. **Allow Buffer Time:** Start your stream a few minutes before the scheduled time to give your audience time to settle in. Use this buffer time to double-check that everything is working properly.

8. **Communicate with Your Community:** Announce the start time of your live stream on your social media, Discord channel, and other relevant platforms. Give them advance notice so they can prepare.

9. **Stay Relaxed and Positive:** Before hitting the "Start Stream" button, take a moment to relax and focus. Maintain a positive and confident attitude during the broadcast.

10. **Have a Backup Plan:** Consider backup solutions in case issues arise during the live stream. For example, if your internet connection drops, do you have a Plan B, like a mobile hotspot?

11. **Plan for Interactive Moments:** If you plan to interact with viewers, have a strategy for integrating that smoothly into your live stream. Prepare questions or discussion topics to encourage engagement.

12. **Set a Clear End Time:** Inform your audience about the expected duration of the live stream and the time you plan to wrap up. This helps viewers plan accordingly.

13. **Record Your Stream:** If desired, set your streaming software to automatically record your live stream. This can be useful for creating content to share later.

Thorough preparation before each live stream is key to ensuring that your viewers enjoy a high-quality experience. The more organized and ready you are, the less stressed you'll be during the live broadcast. Once everything is in place, you can focus on creating exceptional content and interacting with your audience.

How to Interact with Live Viewers

Interacting live with viewers is one of the most important features of streaming. It allows you to connect with your audience, strengthen community loyalty, and provide a more engaging viewing experience. Here are some tips on how to effectively interact with live viewers:

1. **Greet Viewers:** At the beginning of the broadcast, take the time to greet viewers as they join. Use their usernames if possible, as this shows you are attentive.

2. **Respond to Live Comments:** Continuously monitor the live chat and respond to comments and questions from viewers. When responding, mention the user's name for a more personal interaction.

3. **Ask Viewers Questions:** Encourage viewers to participate by asking them questions. For example, ask for their opinions on a topic you're discussing or on a decision you need to make.

4. **Engage with Donations and Subscriptions:** Actively thank viewers who donate or subscribe to your channel. You can personalize your thanks based on the donation amount or subscription duration.

5. **Hold Q&A Sessions:** Occasionally dedicate part of your stream to a Q&A session. Viewers enjoy asking questions and learning more about you.

6. **Engage in Conversations:** Encourage live discussions by bringing up interesting topics and inviting viewers to share their opinions. Stay open to differing viewpoints.

7. **Interact with Newcomers:** When new viewers join your stream, take a moment to warmly welcome them. This encourages them to stay and engage in the chat.

8. **Use Polls:** You can use live polls to allow viewers to vote on gameplay choices, content, or other relevant decisions.

9. **Invite Viewers to Play with You:** If you're playing video games, occasionally invite viewers to join you for online games. This strengthens interaction with your audience.

10. **Create a Positive Environment:** Ensure that the live chat remains respectful and free from

harassment. Moderate the chat as needed to maintain a positive atmosphere.

11. **Ask for Audience Feedback:** Encourage your viewers to give feedback on your content and live stream. Their comments can help you improve.

12. **Be Authentic:** Sincerity and authenticity are essential for creating a real connection with your audience. Be yourself and show interest in your viewers.

13. **Stay Focused on the Game or Content:** While it's important to interact with viewers, don't let it distract you excessively from the game or content you are streaming. Find a balance.

14. **Use Animations and Effects:** To make interactions more visual, use animations, alerts, and special effects in response to donations, subscriptions, and viewer actions.

15. **Analyze Comments and Reactions:** After the stream, take time to review viewer comments and reactions. This can provide valuable insights for improving your future broadcasts.

Live interaction with viewers is a dynamic aspect of streaming that can greatly enhance your experience and that of your audience. Be active, engaging, and respectful towards your community to build strong connections and create a memorable viewing experience.

Managing Technical Issues

When streaming live, it is inevitable that you will occasionally encounter technical issues. Effectively managing these problems is crucial for maintaining a quality viewing experience and minimizing disruptions for your audience. Here are some tips for handling technical issues during your live streams:

1. **Be Prepared:** Before each broadcast, ensure that all your equipment is functioning properly. Conduct audio and video tests to detect potential problems. Also, ensure that your internet connection is stable.

2. **Have a Backup Plan:** Consider backup solutions in case something goes wrong. For example, if your internet connection is interrupted, have a mobile hotspot ready to use. If your camera fails, have a backup camera.

3. **Inform Your Audience:** If you encounter a technical issue during the live stream, don't hide it from your audience. Quickly inform them of the situation and let them know you

are working to resolve it. Transparency builds trust.

4. **Stay Calm:** When faced with a technical issue, remain calm and professional. Panic can worsen the situation. Your positive attitude can help reassure your audience.

5. **Modify Plans if Necessary:** If the technical issue is serious and cannot be resolved quickly, consider altering your streaming plans. You might announce that you will postpone the stream or address another topic while waiting for the issue to be resolved.

6. **Test Before Streaming:** If you plan to introduce new features, software updates, or new hardware, conduct thorough tests before the live stream to avoid unpleasant surprises.

7. **Have Technical Support:** If possible, have someone available to help you troubleshoot technical issues during the stream. This could be a moderator or a friend who can offer advice in case of problems.

8. **Record Your Stream:** If you fear that technical issues may disrupt your broadcast, consider simultaneously recording the stream on your

computer. This way, you can upload a version without issues later.

9. **Analyze Problems After the Stream:** After each broadcast, take the time to examine what happened. Identify the causes of the technical problems and look for ways to prevent them in the future.

10. **Upgrade Your Equipment:** If you frequently encounter technical problems, consider investing in higher-quality equipment. Reliable hardware reduces the risk of failures.

11. **Be Ready to Learn:** Technical problems are often a learning opportunity. Use each issue as a chance to improve your technical skills and crisis management.

Managing technical issues is an integral part of live streaming. Experienced streamers know that it's not a matter of "if" but "when" a problem will occur. By being prepared, transparent, and professional in handling these issues, you can minimize their impact on your live stream and maintain audience satisfaction.

Chapter 6

Monetization and Revenue

The Different Sources of Income for Streamers (Subscriptions, Donations, Advertisements, etc.)

In this chapter, we will explore the various sources of income available to streamers. Monetizing your streaming channel can be essential to support your passion and hard work. Here's an overview of the main sources of income for streamers:

The Different Sources of Income for Streamers:

1. **Subscriptions:** Subscriptions are one of the main sources of income for streamers on platforms like Twitch. Viewers can subscribe to your channel in exchange for various perks, such as custom emotes and access to

subscriber-only chat. Streamers receive a share of subscription revenue, which can provide a stable income source.

2. **Donations:** Donations are direct contributions from your viewers. They can donate money during your live streams. This can be a significant income source, especially if you have a loyal and generous community.

3. **Advertisements:** On some platforms, you can generate revenue by airing advertisements during your live streams. Advertising revenue depends on the number of viewers and the frequency of ads. However, keep in mind that too many ads can discourage viewers.

4. **Affiliates:** Affiliate marketing involves promoting products or services and earning a commission on sales generated through your affiliate links. For example, if you play a video game, you can promote the game using an affiliate link and earn money whenever someone purchases it through your link.

5. **Merchandise Sales:** Many streamers sell merchandise such as t-shirts, mugs, posters, and custom stickers related to their channel. This can be an additional revenue source while reinforcing community loyalty.

6. **Sponsorships:** Sponsorships involve working with brands or companies to promote their products or services during your live streams. In return, you receive compensation or free products. Sponsorships can be a lucrative revenue source for popular streamers.

7. **Memberships on Other Platforms:** If you also create content on other platforms, such as YouTube, Patreon, or OnlyFans, you can generate additional income through subscriptions, donations, and sponsored videos on these platforms.

8. **Courses and Coaching:** If you have specific skills related to streaming, gaming, or other areas, you can offer paid courses or coaching sessions to interested viewers.

9. **Special Events and Fundraising:** Organize special events, streaming marathons, or charity fundraisers to encourage viewers to donate or subscribe.

10. **Paid Resources:** If you create guides, tutorials, presets, or other useful resources for other streamers, you can sell them online.

It's important to note that monetizing streaming takes time and largely depends on the size of your audience and your commitment to your community. It is advisable to diversify your income sources to reduce financial risks. Additionally, be transparent with your audience about how you generate income to maintain their trust.

Establishing Partnerships and Negotiating Contracts

Establishing partnerships and negotiating contracts are important steps for streamers looking to develop their careers and increase their revenue. Partnerships can take various forms, including agreements with brands, gaming companies, other streamers, and even streaming platforms themselves. Here's how you can approach this strategy and some tips for success:

Why Establishing Partnerships is Important:

1. **Increased Revenue Potential:** Partnerships can be very lucrative. Brands and companies are often willing to pay to be associated with popular and influential streamers.

2. **Access to Resources:** Partnerships can give you access to resources and perks you wouldn't have otherwise. This can include free gaming equipment, promotional

products, or even invitations to exclusive events.

3. **Audience Growth:** Partnering with other streamers or streaming platforms can help you reach new audiences. You can collaborate with similar streamers for joint streams or get promoted on a broader platform.

4. **Increased Credibility and Visibility:** Partnerships with reputable brands or gaming companies can enhance your credibility as a streamer. This can also increase your visibility in the streaming industry.

Tips for Establishing Partnerships and Negotiating Contracts:

1. **Build Your Audience First:** Most partnerships are offered to streamers who already have an established audience. Focus on growing your community before seeking partnerships.

2. **Identify Potential Partners:** Look for brands, gaming companies, streamers, or platforms that align with your niche and values.

Partnerships should be relevant to your audience.

3. **Create a Media Kit:** Prepare a professional media kit that highlights your achievements, audience, streaming statistics, previous collaborations, and any other relevant information. This can help you stand out during partnership outreach.

4. **Contact Companies Professionally:** When reaching out to brands or companies, be professional and well-informed about their products or services. Clearly explain how you can mutually benefit from a partnership.

5. **Know Your Worth:** Have a realistic idea of your content and influence's value. Don't underestimate your worth when negotiating contracts.

6. **Read Contracts Carefully:** Before signing a contract, make sure you understand all terms and conditions. If necessary, consult a lawyer specializing in the streaming industry for advice.

7. **Negotiate Smartly:** Don't accept the first contract offered to you. Negotiate smartly to secure terms that suit you. This can include compensation, obligations, partnership duration, etc.

8. **Be Transparent with Your Audience:** When making a promotion or a partnership collaboration, always inform your audience that you were compensated or received benefits. Transparency is key to maintaining your community's trust.

9. **Be Professional:** Be professional in all your interactions with potential and existing partners. Meet deadlines and fulfill contract obligations.

10. **Follow Up:** After establishing a partnership, regularly follow up with your partners to ensure all parties are satisfied and goals are being met.

Partnerships can be an exciting avenue for streamers to increase their revenue, enhance their credibility, and broaden their audience. However, it's essential to remain selective and ensure that partnerships align with your goals and values as a streamer.

Financial Management for Streamers

Financial management is a crucial component of long-term success as a streamer. While streaming can be a lucrative source of income, it's important to manage your finances wisely to ensure financial stability, plan for the future, and avoid financial issues. Here are some tips for effective financial management as a streamer:

1. **Establish a Budget:** Start by creating a clear budget that accounts for your income and expenses. This will help you keep track of your money, avoid overspending, and save for the future.

2. **Separate Personal and Business Finances:** It's essential to maintain a clear separation between your personal finances and those related to streaming. Having a separate bank account for your streaming activities will make financial management easier.

3. **Pay Your Taxes:** As a streamer, you're considered a self-employed worker in many jurisdictions. Be sure to understand your tax obligations and set aside a portion of your income to pay your taxes. Consult a tax professional for appropriate advice.

4. **Create an Emergency Fund:** Since streamer incomes can be irregular, it's wise to establish an emergency fund to cover unforeseen expenses, such as equipment repairs or medical costs.

5. **Diversify Your Income Sources:** Don't rely solely on streaming income. Diversify your income sources by exploring other opportunities such as partnerships, affiliations, merchandise sales, sponsorships, etc.

6. **Save for the Future:** Consider saving and investing a portion of your income for the future. Building retirement savings is a prudent financial step.

7. **Manage Your Expenses:** Be mindful of your personal and business expenses. Avoid impulse purchases and spend thoughtfully. Keep an eye on recurring costs such as subscriptions to software or streaming services.

8. **Keep Accurate Financial Records:** Maintain accurate records of your income and expenses. This will facilitate tax management and help you understand your financial situation.

9. **Consult a Professional:** If you're unsure how to manage your finances as a streamer, consider consulting an accountant or financial advisor. They can help you develop a financial strategy tailored to your situation.

10. **Plan for the Long Term:** Develop a long-term financial plan that takes into account your personal and professional goals. This can include purchasing equipment, expanding your channel, preparing for low-income periods, etc.

Responsible financial management is essential to ensuring the sustainability of your streaming career. By adopting healthy financial habits, investing in your future, and staying aware of your spending, you can ensure that streaming remains a positive and sustainable source of income.

Chapter 7
Evolution as a Streamer

The Importance of Constant Improvement

1. **Satisfying Your Audience**: Your audience expects you to deliver quality content. By striving to improve, you can meet their expectations and maintain their interest.

2. **Staying Competitive:** The streaming industry is highly competitive. Streamers who work on improving themselves have an edge over those who stagnate. This can help you attract new viewers and stand out.

3. **Adapting to Trends:** Viewer trends and preferences evolve. By keeping an eye on new trends, popular games, and changes on streaming platforms, you can adjust your content to stay relevant.

4. **Skill Development:** Improving as a streamer also helps you develop valuable skills such as communication, marketing, time management, and problem-solving, which can be beneficial in other areas of your life.

5. **Community Loyalty:** Streamers who invest in their improvement show their community that they care about their experience. This can strengthen viewer loyalty and encourage ongoing support.

How You Can Constantly Improve:

1. **Evaluation and Feedback:** Take the time to regularly assess your own content. Also, ask for honest feedback from your audience. Use this information to identify areas for improvement.

2. **Training and Learning:** Invest in your own development by attending training sessions, reading books about streaming, taking online courses, and networking with experienced streamers.

3. **Reviewing Your Content Plan:** Regularly revisit your content plan and adjust it based on current trends and your audience's interests. Experiment with new content types to diversify your channel.

4. **Collaborations and Partnerships:** Working with other streamers or content creators can help you **acquire new skills and gain valuable insights.**

5. **Analyzing Your Statistics:** Use the data and statistics available on streaming platforms to understand what works and what doesn't. Identify your channel's highlights and areas that need improvement.

6. **Setting Goals:** Establish clear and achievable goals to measure your progress. This can include audience growth goals, financial goals, or quality-related objectives.

7. **Participating in Events and Competitions:** Engaging in special events, gaming competitions, or streaming challenges can push you out of your comfort zone and improve your skills.

8. **Being Open to Constructive Criticism:** Don't take criticism personally. Be open to constructive feedback from your audience and other streamers. Use these critiques to improve.

9. **Staying Passionate:** Passion is a powerful driver of constant improvement. Continue to love what you do and seek new ways to make it even better.

Constant improvement is essential for success in the streaming world. It allows you to stay competitive, build community loyalty, and achieve your goals as a streamer. By investing in your development and remaining open to change, you can continue to grow and thrive as a streaming content creator.

Using Feedback and Statistics to Improve

One of the most effective ways for a streamer to constantly improve is to gather feedback and analyze their channel's statistics. Audience feedback and statistical data provide essential insights into what works well on your channel and what can be improved. Here's how you can use this information to refine your streaming skills:

1. **Collect Feedback**:

    o   Actively encourage your audience to leave comments during your live broadcasts. Ask open-ended questions to spark responses and invite viewers to share their opinions.

    o   Create a welcoming environment where viewers feel comfortable sharing their feedback, whether it's positive or negative.

    o   Utilize social media, forums, and discussion platforms to gather additional feedback outside of your live streams.

- Take feedback constructively. Avoid taking criticism personally and use it as a learning opportunity.

2. **Analyze Your Channel's Statistics:**

- Use the analytical tools provided by the streaming platform you are using. These tools can give you insights into viewer counts, watch time, subscriptions, donations, etc.

- Regularly examine your statistics to identify trends and patterns. Look for key performance indicators that help you understand what works and what doesn't.

- Compare the performance of different videos or live broadcasts to determine what attracts the most audience and generates the highest engagement.

- Identify highlights from your live streams, such as audience peaks or high engagement rates, and analyze what triggered them. Use this information to replicate those successes.

3. **Adjust Your Content and Strategy:**

o Based on feedback and statistics, make adjustments to your content and streaming style. For example, if viewers particularly enjoy a certain type of content, consider producing more of it.

o Test new ideas and formats to see how your audience reacts. Be open to experimentation to find out what works best for your channel.

o If you notice certain elements of your broadcast or channel are less popular, consider improving or eliminating them to focus your resources on what works.

o Use feedback to refine your communication with your audience. Be responsive to questions and concerns to maintain high engagement levels.

o Set goals based on your feedback and statistical data. For instance, if you find that your audience enjoys your Q&A sessions, plan more of them into your live streams.

4. **Avoid Stagnation:**

- Even if you are successful as a streamer, avoid resting on your laurels. The ongoing growth of your channel depends on your ability to remain adaptable and continuously improve.

- Stay attuned to your audience and industry trends. What works today may no longer be relevant tomorrow.

- Continue to invest in your own development by attending training, exploring new skills, and collaborating with other streamers.

By proactively using audience feedback and your channel's statistics, you can refine your content, attract more viewers, and strengthen your engagement. Constant improvement is key to succeeding as a streamer in a constantly evolving competitive environment.

Skill Development in Streaming

Skill development is a crucial element for any streamer who wants to succeed in the streaming world. Constantly improving your skills allows you to create higher quality content, retain your audience, and achieve your goals as a content creator. Here are some essential skills every streamer should seek to develop:

1. **Communication Skills**:

   o **Oral Communication**: Verbal communication is at the heart of streaming. Work on your articulation, voice tone, and clarity to make your live broadcasts more enjoyable to watch.

   o **Audience Interaction**: Learning to engage effectively with your audience is essential. Ask questions, respond to comments, and create an interactive environment for your viewers.

2. **Technical Skills**:

- Equipment Mastery: Understand how your equipment works, from cameras to microphones and streaming software. Learn how to troubleshoot common technical issues.

- Software Proficiency: Familiarize yourself with streaming and video editing software. The more you master these tools, the more you can customize and enhance the quality of your content.

- Stream Optimization: Learn how to optimize your streaming settings, such as resolution, bitrate, and refresh rates, to provide a smooth visual experience for your audience.

3. Entertainment Skills:

- Storytelling: Develop the ability to tell captivating stories or commentate gameplay entertainingly. Effective storytelling can keep viewers engaged.

- Humor: Humor can be a valuable asset in entertaining your audience. Work on your sense of humor and responsiveness to comedic situations to make your content more appealing.

4. **Time Management Skills**:

   o **Planning**: Learn to plan your live streams and content in advance. Effective planning can help you stay consistent and avoid interruptions.

   o **Scheduling Management**: Streaming can be time-consuming. Develop time management skills to balance your daily life with your streaming career.

5. **Marketing Skills**:

   o **Promotion**: Learn how to promote your streaming channel on social media, forums, and other platforms to attract new viewers.

   o **Branding**: Create a cohesive brand identity with an appealing logo, banner, and channel description. Strong branding can help you stand out.

6. **Community Management Skills**:

   o **Moderation**: If you have a large audience, chat moderation can become a challenge. Learn to manage moderators and establish clear rules for your community.

- o **Comment Management**: Be able to manage both positive and negative comments professionally and respectfully.

7. **Analytical Skills**:

- o **Statistical Analysis**: Use the statistical data provided by streaming platforms to evaluate your channel's performance and make informed decisions for improvement.

- o **Self-Evaluation**: Learn to watch your own broadcasts and identify areas where you can improve. Be critical and ready to make changes.

Skill development in streaming is an ongoing process. The more you invest in your own development, the better quality content you can provide, the more you can retain your audience, and the closer you can get to achieving your goals as a streamer. Ultimately, streaming is a combination of technical skills, entertainment, and community management, and mastering these skills can help you succeed in this competitive industry.

Chapter 8

Challenges and Pitfalls to Avoid

Legal Issues and Copyright

1. **Copyright on Music**: Using copyrighted music in your live streams can lead to copyright claims or bans. To avoid this, use royalty-free music or obtain the necessary licenses.

2. **Copyright on Video Games**: Video games are subject to copyright, and streaming a game without permission can pose problems. Most game developers allow live streaming, but it's important to check the policies for each game you plan to stream.

3. **Right to Image and Privacy**: If you stream from public places or film people without their consent, you may violate their right to image and privacy. Make sure to obtain appropriate permissions if necessary.

4. **Trademarks and Logos**: Using trademarks and logos in your live streams can lead to legal issues related to intellectual property rights. Avoid using trademarks without permission.

5. **Offensive or Illegal Content**: Streaming offensive, illegal, or inappropriate content can lead to legal sanctions, broadcast bans, and a damaged

reputation. Always adhere to current rules and laws.

Tips for Avoiding Legal Issues and Copyright:

1. **Know the Law**: Familiarize yourself with copyright laws, rights to image and privacy, and other laws applicable to your streaming activities in your jurisdiction.

2. **Obtain Permissions**: If you need to use copyrighted content, such as music, obtain the appropriate licenses or use royalty-free tracks.

3. **Respect Game Policies**: Before streaming a video game, check the live streaming policies of the developer or publisher to ensure you comply with their terms.

4. **Informed Consent**: When streaming from public places or filming people, obtain their informed consent to avoid issues related to image rights and privacy.

5. **Content Moderation**: Make sure to moderate the content you stream and ensure it complies with the rules of the streaming platform you are using.

6. **Be Responsible**: Ensure that you stream respectful and lawful content. Avoid promoting or participating in illegal activities.

7. **Consult a Professional**: If you have questions or concerns regarding legal issues, consult a lawyer

specializing in digital media and streaming for appropriate legal advice.

Legal issues and copyright are serious concerns for streamers. By understanding the laws and adopting responsible practices, you can avoid legal pitfalls and continue to stream with peace of mind. It is essential to be aware of the rules and responsibilities that come with streaming to protect your career and reputation.

Managing Trolls and Harmful Behavior

As an active streamer, it is almost inevitable to encounter trolls and harmful behaviors from time to time. Trolls are individuals who seek to disrupt, provoke, or harass streamers and their online audience. It is important to know how to handle these situations to maintain a positive and healthy live streaming environment. Here are some tips for effectively managing trolls and harmful behaviors:

1. **Ignore Trolls**: In many cases, the best response to a troll is to ignore them. Trolls often seek a reaction, and not giving them the attention they seek can discourage them.

2. **Block and Ban**: Most streaming platforms offer blocking and banning features. Blocking a user means they can no longer send you messages or comment on your channel. Banning a user prevents them from participating in your live streams.

3. **Community Moderation**: Appoint trusted moderators in your community to monitor the chat and remove inappropriate or offensive messages. Moderators can help

maintain a positive live streaming environment.

4. **Establish Community Rules**: Post clear rules for your channel and ensure your audience understands them. The rules should indicate what is allowed and what is not, and specify the consequences for inappropriate behaviors.

5. **Report to Platforms**: Report trolls and harmful behaviors to the platform's moderators. Streaming platforms generally take reports seriously and can take action against users who violate the rules.

6. **Stay Calm and Professional**: When faced with a troll, it is important to remain calm and professional. Do not respond aggressively or offensively, as this can escalate the situation.

7. **Mentally Prepare**: Streaming can sometimes be stressful, especially when dealing with trolls or negative comments. Develop strategies to manage stress, such as meditation or talking with other experienced streamers.

8. **Educate Your Audience**: Take time to explain to your audience that trolls exist, but you prefer to focus your energy on creating a

positive streaming environment. Encourage your community to report harmful behaviors.

9. **Use Chat Filters**: Many streaming platforms offer customizable chat filters. You can set them up to automatically block certain inappropriate keywords or phrases.

10. **Stay Vigilant**: Trolls can be persistent, so continue to monitor the chat and take appropriate action as needed.

It is important to remember that while trolls and harmful behaviors can be disturbing, they should not deter you from pursuing your passion for streaming. By adopting appropriate management strategies and fostering a positive environment, you can continue to create quality content and build a strong community around your streaming channel.

Avoiding Burnout

Streaming can be an exciting and rewarding activity, but it can also be mentally and emotionally demanding. To maintain a healthy streaming career and avoid burnout, it is essential to take steps to care for yourself. Here are some tips for avoiding burnout as a streamer:

1. **Set Regular Streaming Schedules**: Define regular streaming hours that fit your lifestyle. Avoid excessive or irregular streaming, which can lead to fatigue.

2. **Schedule Rest Days**: Regularly take days off where you do not stream. This will allow you to recharge and prevent burnout.

3. **Avoid Overloading Your Schedule**: Do not commit to streaming for too long in one stretch. Excessively long streams can be physically and mentally exhausting.

4. **Take Breaks During Streams**: Schedule short breaks during your streams to stretch, hydrate, and rest briefly. This can help you stay energized and focused.

5. **Diversify Your Content**: Avoid focusing solely on one type of content or game. Diversifying

your content can help prevent boredom and keep your passion alive.

6. **Stay Connected with Reality**: Remember to maintain social relationships outside of streaming. Spend time with friends and family to balance your social life.

7. **Set Realistic Goals**: Avoid putting excessive pressure on yourself by setting unrealistic goals for audience growth or income. Be realistic about your expectations.

8. **Listen to Your Body**: Pay attention to your body's signals. If you feel fatigued, stressed, or show signs of burnout, take them seriously and rest.

9. **Consider Wellness Activities**: Incorporate wellness activities into your routine, such as exercise, meditation, relaxation, or hobbies that help you unwind.

10. **Learn to Say No**: Do not feel obligated to accept every streaming or collaboration request. Learn to say no when you need time for yourself.

11. **Seek a Support Network**: Talk with other streamers or content creators who understand the challenges of streaming. Social support can be valuable.

12. **Consider a Flexible Streaming Pace**: If you feel you are on the brink of burnout, do not hesitate to temporarily reduce your streaming pace or take an extended break if necessary.

Burnout can negatively impact your physical and mental well-being, as well as the quality of your streaming content. It is essential to take care of yourself, set boundaries, and maintain a balance between your passion for streaming and your personal health. By adopting appropriate time and energy management practices, you can continue to enjoy streaming while avoiding the risks of burnout.

Chapter 9
The Future of Streaming

Emerging Trends in the Streaming World

1. **The Rise of Non-Gaming Content:** While video games have been the starting point for streaming, more and more content creators are expanding their focus to include areas like cooking, music, art, fashion, and even education. Streaming non-gaming content is gaining popularity and offers new opportunities for creators.

2. **Augmented Reality (AR) and Virtual Reality (VR):** Augmented and virtual reality technologies are opening exciting new perspectives for streaming. Streamers can create more immersive and interactive experiences using these technologies, whether for VR gaming, live shows, or special events.

3. **Expansion of Streaming Platforms:** In addition to established platforms like Twitch and YouTube Gaming, new platforms are regularly emerging. These new platforms offer streamers the chance to explore new audiences and diversify their revenue streams.

4. **Unique Content Streaming:** Some streamers are turning to the concept of "unique content streaming," where they focus on a specific game or type of content. This can allow for deeper

expertise and stronger engagement with a passionate audience.

5. **Viewer Interactions:** Viewers increasingly want to actively participate in live broadcasts. Trends like polls, challenges, chat commands to influence gameplay, and real-time interactions are gaining popularity.

6. **Diverse Monetization:** Streamers are seeking various sources of income, from subscriptions and donations to brand partnerships, merchandise sales, and creating exclusive content for subscribers.

7. **Importance of Production Quality:** As streaming becomes more professional, production quality becomes crucial. Streamers are investing in better audiovisual equipment, sets, lighting, and video editing to deliver high-quality content.

8. **Regulation and Copyright:** With the growth of streaming, legal and copyright issues are becoming increasingly complex. Platform regulations and policies are evolving, and streamers must be aware of their legal obligations.

9. **Collaborations and Streaming Teams:** Streamers are increasingly collaborating with other content creators, forming streaming teams to share their audience and create special events.

10. **Customization and Branding:** A streamer's brand identity is becoming increasingly important to

stand out. Streamers are investing in customizing their channels, with consistent logos, banners, and themes.

To succeed in the future of streaming, it's essential to take a proactive approach to keep up with trends, adapt to industry changes, and remain creative in how you engage your audience. Streaming will continue to evolve, offering new opportunities for passionate and innovative content creators. By staying informed and adapting your strategy, you can thrive in this ever-changing environment.

Preparing for Technological Evolutions

In the streaming world, staying up to date with technological advancements is essential to maintain the quality of your content, stay competitive, and seize new opportunities. Here's how you can prepare for technological changes as a streamer:

1. **Technology Monitoring:** Regularly stay informed about the latest trends and technological advancements related to streaming. Follow blogs, forums, podcasts, and specialized YouTube channels to keep up.

2. **Equipment Upgrades:** Invest in quality streaming equipment. Continuous improvements in audiovisual technology can significantly enhance the quality of your live broadcasts. This may include better cameras, studio microphones, more powerful computers, and faster Internet connections.

3. **Exploring Virtual and Augmented Reality:** Keep an eye on developments in VR and AR.

These technologies offer increased opportunities for interaction and engagement with your audience.

4. **Experimenting with New Platforms:** Stay open to emerging streaming platforms. You might find new audiences or opportunities on these growing platforms.

5. **Continuous Learning:** Stay engaged in continuous learning. Take online courses, attend streaming conferences, and participate in forums to develop your skills and understanding of the latest technologies.

6. **Adaptability:** Be prepared to adapt your content based on new technologies. For example, if a new live chat or audience interaction feature becomes popular, consider integrating it into your channel.

7. **Bandwidth Management:** As video quality increases, you will need faster Internet bandwidth to stream in high resolution. Ensure you have a stable and fast connection to avoid streaming issues.

8. **Collaboration with Experts:** Don't hesitate to collaborate with technology experts or consultants to help you leverage the latest advancements. They can advise you on best practices and necessary updates.

9. **Long-Term Planning:** Anticipate technological changes by planning for the long term. Your equipment may need to be updated or replaced at regular intervals to remain competitive.

10. **Skill Diversification:** Don't limit yourself to a single skill. Learn various aspects of video production, editing, graphic design, online marketing, etc. The more skills you have, the more versatile you'll be in the face of technological changes.

Ultimately, technology is a key driver of the streaming industry, and those who succeed are those who can effectively embrace it. Be curious, ready to learn and adapt, and use technology to enhance your content and engage with your audience in innovative ways. This will help you thrive in an ever-evolving sector.

Tips for Staying Relevant as a Streamer

In a constantly evolving and growing streaming world, staying relevant is essential to maintain and grow your audience. Here are some tips to help you remain relevant as a streamer:

1. **Be Consistent:** Consistency is one of the keys to success in streaming. Establish a regular streaming schedule and stick to it as much as possible. Your audience will appreciate knowing when you're online.

2. **Diversify Your Content:** Don't limit yourself to one game or type of content. Diversify your content to reach different audiences and avoid burnout.

3. **Stay Updated with Trends:** Keep an eye on popular games and emerging trends. Play trending games and explore new releases to attract a wider audience.

4. **Engage with Your Audience:** Interaction with your audience is essential. Respond to

comments, ask questions, and create an environment where viewers feel valued.

5. **Create Strong Branding:** Develop a solid brand identity for your channel. A logo, banner, consistent design elements, and a distinctive personality will help you stand out.

6. **Invest in Quality:** Audio and video quality are crucial. Invest in good equipment to enhance the quality of your live broadcasts.

7. **Collaborate with Other Streamers:** Collaborating with other streamers can help expand your audience. Look for collaboration opportunities with similar content creators.

8. **Be Active on Social Media:** Use social media to promote your live broadcasts, interact with your audience outside of streams, and share moments from your life.

9. **Listen to Feedback:** Pay attention to your audience's feedback. Ask for constructive criticism and be ready to make improvements based on their suggestions.

10. **Stay Flexible:** Be prepared to adapt to changes. Trends, platforms, and audience preferences can change quickly, so be flexible in your approach.

11. **Keep Learning:** Streaming is a constantly evolving industry. Stay curious, continue learning new skills, and keep up with the latest technological trends.

12. **Provide Added Value:** Look for ways to offer added value to your audience. This could be in the form of gaming tips, entertainment, or interesting information.

13. **Set Goals:** Define clear goals for your streaming channel. Having a long-term objective can motivate you to stay engaged and grow as a streamer.

14. **Stay Authentic:** Be yourself. Your authenticity will attract an audience that connects with you as a person, which can be more sustainable than playing a role.

15. **Manage Your Time Effectively:** Balance your time between live streaming, creating offline content, and your personal life to avoid burnout.

Staying relevant as a streamer takes time, determination, and effort. However, by following these tips and staying engaged in your passion for streaming, you can continue to grow your audience and thrive in the ever-evolving streaming industry.

Chapter 10
Additional
Resources

Useful Tools and Software for Streamers

1. **Streaming Software:**

   o **OBS Studio (Open Broadcaster Software):** This is a popular open-source streaming software for Windows, macOS, and Linux. It offers advanced features for video capture, encoding, and live broadcasting.

   o **Streamlabs OBS:** A customized version of OBS Studio with streamer-specific integrations, including alerts, widgets, and themes.

2. **Game Capture Software:**

   o **NVIDIA ShadowPlay and AMD ReLive:** These software tools are integrated with NVIDIA and AMD graphics cards, respectively, allowing you to record or live stream your gameplay with minimal impact on game performance.

o **Fraps:** A screen and video capture tool that can be useful for capturing gameplay moments.

3. **Video Editing Software:**

o **Adobe Premiere Pro, DaVinci Resolve, Final Cut Pro:** These professional software programs are ideal for editing your streaming videos, adding special effects, and enhancing the overall quality of your content.

4. **Live Chat Software:**

o **Streamlabs Chatbot (AnkhBot):** A customizable chatbot tool that can help manage your live chat, broadcast announcements, create polls, etc.

o **Nightbot:** Another popular chatbot that offers similar moderation and chat interaction features.

5. **Audience Management Tools:**

o **Streamelements and Streamlabs:** These platforms offer comprehensive audience management tools, including customizable alerts, revenue dashboards, and detailed analytics.

6. **Graphics and Design Software:**

o **Adobe Photoshop and Adobe Illustrator:** These software programs are ideal for creating custom graphics, logos, banners, overlays, and other visual elements for your streaming channel.

- o **Canva:** A user-friendly online design tool for creating quality streaming visuals without advanced graphic design skills.

7. **Communication Tools:**

- o **Discord:** A voice and text chat platform that can be used to create a community around your streaming channel and interact with your audience outside of live broadcasts.

- o **Zoom and Skype:** These video conferencing tools can be useful for collaborations with other streamers or for live interviews.

8. **Social Media Management Software:**

- o **Buffer, Hootsuite:** Use these tools to schedule and automate your social media posts, allowing you to maintain a consistent online presence.

9. **Analytics and Tracking:**

- o **Google Analytics and Twitch Analytics:** Use these tools to track your channel's performance, including broadcast statistics, engagement rates, and growth trends.

Using these tools and software wisely can simplify the streaming process, improve the quality of your content, and enhance your engagement with your audience. Choose the tools that best fit your needs and streaming style to create a more effective and enjoyable streaming experience.

Online Communities and Forums for Streamers

One of the most valuable resources for streamers is the ability to connect with other content creators, share tips, get answers to their questions, and find support. Online communities and forums dedicated to streamers play an essential role in this regard. Here's why they are important and some of the most popular community spaces for streamers:

1. **Knowledge Sharing:** Online communities allow streamers to share their expertise and learn from others. You can get advice on technical setup, audience growth, channel management, and much more.

2. **Emotional Support:** Streaming can be a lonely venture, but online communities offer a space where streamers can emotionally support each other. You can share your successes, challenges, and concerns with people who understand your experiences.

3. **Cross-Promotion:** Forums and communities are excellent places to promote your streaming channel and establish collaborations with other streamers. You can share your live broadcast links and discover new audiences.

4. **Problem Solving:** If you encounter technical issues or challenges related to streaming, forums are a great place to ask questions. Other experienced streamers can offer solutions and tips to resolve your issues.

5. **Networking:** Forums and communities are perfect for expanding your professional network. You can meet people working in the streaming industry, including channel moderators, game developers, and brand representatives.

Here are some of the popular online communities and forums for streamers:

1. **Reddit (r/Twitch and r/SmallStreamers):** Reddit hosts several communities dedicated to streaming, including r/Twitch and r/SmallStreamers. You can ask questions, share your successes, and interact with other streamers.

2. **Discord:** Many streaming channels and content creators have their own Discord servers, where they interact with their audience outside of live broadcasts. You can also join Discord servers of popular streamers to expand your network.

3. **Twitch Community:** The streaming platform itself has a community section where you can find streamers, moderators, and viewers. It's a great place to discover new content creators.

4. **Twitter:** Although Twitter isn't a forum per se, it's a major platform for promoting streaming and interacting with other streamers. Use streaming-related hashtags to find relevant conversations.

5. **TwitchCon:** This is an annual convention hosted by Twitch, where streamers gather to share their experiences, participate in workshops, and make connections.

6. **Technical Support Forums:** Forums such as the Twitch support forums or OBS Studio forums are specifically dedicated to troubleshooting technical issues related to streaming.

7. **YouTube Communities:** If you stream on YouTube, video comments and discussions in

the "About" section of your channel are places where you can interact with your audience.

Ultimately, participating in online communities and forums for streamers can help you grow as a content creator, solve problems, build connections, and find valuable support. Don't hesitate to explore these spaces to enrich your streaming experience.

Books, Videos, and Other Resources for Expanding Your Knowledge

Continuous learning is essential to remain competent as a streamer and to constantly improve your content. Here are some types of resources you can use to deepen your knowledge about streaming:

1. **Books:**

   o **"Streaming 101: The Ultimate Guide to Twitch and YouTube Live" by Justin Pot:** This book provides a comprehensive guide for beginners on Twitch and YouTube Live, covering everything from technical setup to content creation.

   o **"Streaming for Gamers" by Ember Kitts:** This book focuses on the practical aspects of streaming, including hardware, software, and best practices for attracting and retaining an audience.

2. **YouTube Channels and Educational Videos:**

   o Several content creators on YouTube offer educational videos on streaming. Look for channels such as "Harris Heller" (Alpha Gaming), "EposVox," and "Gaming Careers" for tutorials and tips on streaming.

3. **Blogs and Online Articles:**

   o Many blogs and websites regularly publish articles on streaming, new trends, and tips. Follow blogs like "Streamer's Haven" and "The Streamer Journal" to stay updated.

4. **Podcasts:**

   o Podcasts like "Stream Key Podcast" offer in-depth discussions and interviews with experienced streamers, which can help you learn more about their journeys and best practices.

5. **Platform Guides:**

   o Streaming platforms such as Twitch and YouTube Gaming provide guides and articles for beginner streamers. Explore these resources to understand policies, features, and best practices specific to each platform.

6. **Online Courses and Training:**

   o Some platforms offer paid or free online courses on streaming. This may include courses on content creation, promotion, and managing your channel.

7. **Books on Related Skills:**

   o To improve your streaming, it may be useful to develop related skills such as marketing, project management, communication, and video editing. Look for books on these topics to enhance your skills.

8. **Books on Psychology and Communication:**

   o Understanding audience psychology and improving your communication skills can have a significant impact on your streaming. Explore books on persuasion psychology, effective communication, and managing online interactions.

9. **Books on Content Creation:**

   o If you want to create more creative and engaging content, books on storytelling, artistic creation, and game design can be helpful.

10. **Online Marketing Courses:**

    o Learning the basics of online marketing can help you promote your streaming channel more effectively. There are many online courses available on platforms like Coursera, Udemy, and LinkedIn Learning.

Remember that streaming is a constantly evolving business, and it's essential to remain curious and open to learning. By exploring these resources, you can acquire new skills, discover helpful tips, and stay at the forefront of the streaming industry.

Conclusion

Encouragement to Persist and Improve as a Streamer

As a streamer, you have embarked on an exciting and demanding journey in the world of online content creation. You have discovered how to share your passion, skills, and interests with a global audience. While this journey may be fraught with challenges, it is also filled with incredible opportunities to grow as a content creator, build a community, and even make a living.

Like any creative endeavor, perseverance is key. You will encounter moments of doubt, technical challenges, fluctuations in audience size, and periods of frustration. However, every obstacle you overcome, every improvement you make to your channel, and every positive interaction with your audience brings you closer to your goals.

Always remember these encouragements to persevere and improve as a streamer:

1. **Learn from Every Experience:** Every live stream, every uploaded video, and every

interaction with your audience is an opportunity to learn and grow. Evaluate what works and what doesn't, and adapt your strategy accordingly.

2. **Be Authentic:** Your authenticity is one of your greatest strengths as a streamer. Stay true to yourself, share your passion enthusiastically, and create a space where viewers feel welcome.

3. **Develop Your Skills:** Streaming encompasses a wide range of skills, from content creation to channel management and promotion. Be prepared to invest time in developing these skills.

4. **Set Goals:** Establish clear goals for your streaming channel. Whether it's reaching a certain number of regular viewers, becoming a platform partner, or collaborating with other streamers, defined goals help you stay focused and motivated.

5. **Stay Open to Growth:** Be ready to evolve as a streamer. The streaming world is constantly changing, and your ability to adapt and innovate can make the difference between success and stagnation.

6. **Don't Forget the Fun:** Above all, streaming should be enjoyable. Don't lose sight of the

passion that brought you here. The more fun you have, the more it will reflect in your content and interactions with your audience.

7. **Seek Support:** Don't underestimate the importance of support from the streamer community. Participate in forums, join Discord servers, and collaborate with other content creators. Peer support can help you overcome challenges and stay motivated.

8. **Stay Persistent:** Success in streaming takes time. Growing your channel and building a loyal audience are processes that require patience and perseverance. Don't be discouraged by periods of low visibility or stagnation.

Remember that every streamer started with humble beginnings, but with hard work, determination, and a positive attitude, you can achieve your goals as a content creator. Keep learning, improving, and sharing your passion with the world. Your journey as a streamer is an ongoing adventure, and the path you take is just as important as the destination. Happy streaming, and good luck with all your future broadcasts!